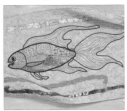

Suppliers - Most stores carry an excellent assortment of supplies. Ask your local store to contact the following companies.

Pens, Inks, Markers
SAKURA - www.sakuraofamerica.com
BIC - www.bicworld.com
COPIC - www.copicmarker.com
MARVY - www.marvy.com
JACQUARD - www.jacquardproducts.com

PENTEL - www.pentelstore.com
PRISMACOLOR - www.prismacolor.com
SHARPIE - www.sharpie.com
TSUKINEKO - www.tsukineko.com

Stabilizer and Fusible Web
SULKY - www.sulky.com
MISTY FUSE - www.softexpressions.com
TIMTEX - www.softexpressions.com

Textile Medium and Textile Paint
GOLDEN - www.goldenartistpaints.com
JOSONJA'S - www.josonja.net
SETACOLOR -
www.dharmatrading.com
JACQUARD -
www.jacquardproducts.com
LIQUITEX - www.liquitex.com

Computer Transfer Sheets
DHARMA -
www.dharmatradingco.com
JACQUARD -
www.jacquardproducts.com
LESLIE RILEY -
www.lesleyriley.com

Tangled Purse

by Mickey Weitsen, CZT

Fabric pens enable you to decorate a number of surfaces with your favorite tangles. A close look at this purse reveals checkerboards, parallel lines, zigzag lines, scallops, swirls, leaves, circles, and an assortment of plant-inspired shapes. Shading gives the piece depth and attractive contrast. This technique works well on hats, shoes and T-shirts, too.

See basic instructions for drawing 'tangles' on pages 22 - 27.

SIZE: 7¾" x 9¼"

MATERIALS
Purchased muslin purse
Sakura Pigma Micron 01 Archival black permanent ink pen
Pencil
Paper stump for shading (or use your finger)
Heavy interfacing
Optional: Scotchgard™

INSTRUCTIONS:
Draw 'tangles' onto the purse.
Shade with a pencil and blend as desired with a paper stump or with your finger.
If you spray your work with Scotchgard, hold the can at least 14" away so a fine mist reaches the fabric; any closer and the ink will bleed.
INTERFACING: Cut 2 layers of interfacing to fit inside the purse. Sew the layers together.
Tack the interfacing inside the purse to prevent sagging.

Marion 'Mickey' Tynan Weitsen

Mickey produces functional pottery and is an experienced calligrapher.

"My exploration of the art of Zentangle® as a Certified Zentangle Teacher (CZT) has prompted me to draw the intricate patterns onto fabric - including purses, scarves, visors and tote bags. Permanent archival Micron pens allow me to create unique and functional multimedia art."

Mickey is from Louisiana. She teaches classes and can be reached at mandhtanglers@yahoo.com.

"I love to begin my tangles in one area... I draw a pattern in a section, then choose another pattern for the second section.

As I add tangles to each area, the design whispers ideas for what to draw in the next section."

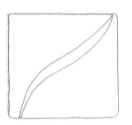

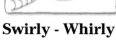

Swirly - Whirly　　　　**Frond**

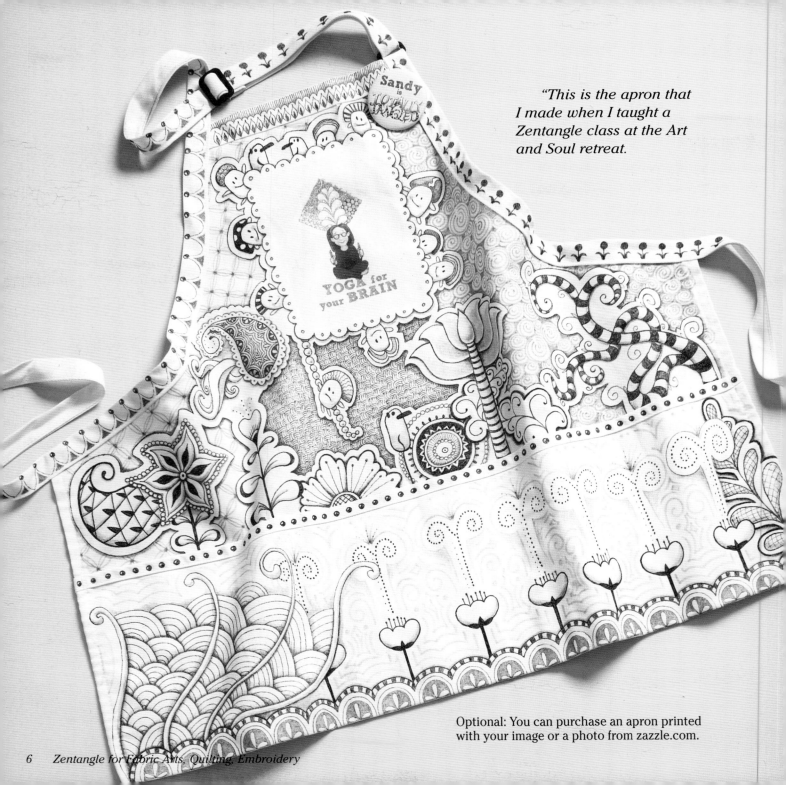

"This is the apron that I made when I taught a Zentangle class at the Art and Soul retreat.

Sandy is TOTALLY TANGLED

YOGA for your BRAIN

Optional: You can purchase an apron printed with your image or a photo from zazzle.com.

Tangled Apron

by Sandy Steen Bartholomew, CZT

Zentangle is all about relaxing your brain so your creativity can get out! Don't overthink your project. Just start... and let it go where it wants to go.

MATERIALS
Purchased muslin apron
Pentel 'Gel Roller for Fabric' pens (for drawing)
Marvy Fabric Marker, light gray (#622 for shading)
Optional: Scotchgard

INSTRUCTIONS:
It helps to pre-wash the apron to remove sizing before starting. I used the features of the apron - the printed image, pockets, ties, etc. as my "strings" and then used a pencil to lightly divide up any large empty expanses.

I find it easiest to start drawing along the edges and around the features.

I used 6 Pentel fabric pens to draw all the tangles. The canvas seems to absorb a lot more ink than a standard T-shirt, so I used a lot of pens to cover the entire surface. I used a Marvy Fabric Marker to do the shading and a bunch of the tangles as well.

The Pentel pen just glides over the surface - and doesn't bleed through - until all the ink is used up. The Marvy pen does bleed, so put a piece of cardboard under the fabric while using it. Also, the gel pen doesn't need the fabric to be stretched to work well.

TIP: Always start with your largest design elements. They break up the surface, provide a focus point and give the illusion that everything else is in the background.

Sandy Steen Bartholomew

Sandy is an author, illustrator, mixed-media artist, and a Certified Zentangle Teacher (CZT). She loves all things creative. Sandy designs and teaches workshops at creative art retreats. She runs a creativity store (Wingdoodle), a mini gallery (The Beehive), has a creative studio (BeezInk Studio), a teaching studio (The Belfry) and an Etsy shop (Bumblebat). Sandy teaches at 'Art and Soul' retreats and has authored two wonderful books about Zentangle... "Totally Tangled" & "AlphaTangle".

Visit her website at www.beezinkstudio.com.

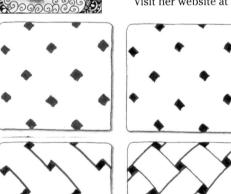

W2* *original Zentangle design **Keeko*** *original Zentangle design

Pieced Quilt

by Vicki Murray, CZT

Writing on fabric with a micron pen is much easier when you stabilize it. I prefer Sticky stabilizer because I am frugal with my supplies and Sticky can be reused several times.

I also discovered that the fabric tends to suck the ink from the pen. Using a light touch and trading out pens regularly makes the drawing easier. It's better to draw twice lightly than once heavily.

I know it sounds funny, but I found myself holding my breath as I drew. When I started to consciously breathe, my shoulders relaxed and I began to enjoy the process.

You will be much happier with the result if you don't try to pre-plan. Just let the design blossom from your imagination.

See basic instructions for drawing 'tangles' on pages 22 - 27.

SIZE: 18" x 18"
MATERIALS
Solid cotton (black, white)
Sakura Micron 01 pens (black, gold)
Pencil for shading
Black-white striped piping (I made mine)
Sulky Sticky heavy-duty stabilizer
    or freezer paper
Batting & backing
Sewing machine, needle, thread

INSTRUCTIONS:
Cut 4 white 6" squares. Apply stabilizer to the back of each square.
Draw the tangles and shade as desired. Remove the stabilizer.
Sew the pieces together using 2" sashings.
Optional: I surrounded each square and the outer edge with striped
    piping for effect.
Layer the top (right side up), backing (wrong side up) and batting.
Sew around the edge leaving an opening for turning.
Turn the piece right side out. Press.
Sew the opening closed.
Quilt as desired. I quilted a simple square around each block
    and around the outer edge creating a frame for the tangles.

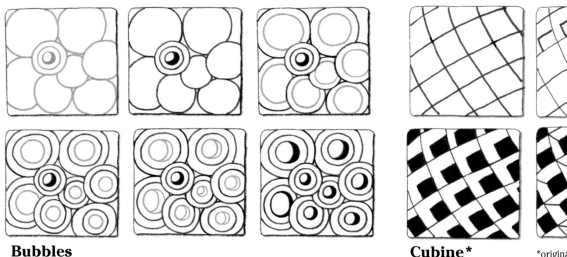

Bubbles　　　　　　　　　　　　　　　　　**Cubine*** 　　**original Zentangle design*

Why make fabric postcards? If you are like me, you have a growing list of fabulous ideas just waiting for the right project, but who has the time to get to them all?

The beauty of making fabric postcards is that you can try a wide variety of fiber art techniques to see what can be achieved without a large investment of time or precious supplies and in the end you will have wonderful little works of art to share with family and friends.

"I love designing with fabric. It's thrilling to take an ivory color fabric like muslin or batik, and add color. It makes the design come alive in a special way!"

See basic instructions for drawing 'tangles' on pages 22 - 27.

Fabric Postcard Basics

SIZE: 4" x 6"

MATERIALS

Off white fabric for the front (you will be drawing and painting on the fabric)
Cardstock or fabric for the back
Sakura black Micron Pen 01
    or *Sharpie* Ultra-Fine permanent marker
JoSonja's Textile Medium
Textile paints (*Pebeo* Setacolor transparent & *Jacquard* Opaque)
Tsukineko all-purpose ink (as desired)
Prismacolor pencils
5" x 7" *Timtex* stabilizer
3" x 5" of fusible web
Freezer paper
Teflon pressing sheet
Sewing machine, needle and thread

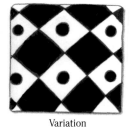

Knightsbridge*   Variation
              *original Zentangle design

Tangle a Postcard
by Jill Buckley

DRAW A PATTERN - Fabric postcards have a top layer, a middle stabilizer, and a backing, exactly like a quilt. • Using a dry iron, press freezer paper to the wrong side of your top fabric to stabilize the piece and make it easy to draw upon. Using a light box or a sunny window, lightly trace the outline drawing onto your fabric with a pencil. Using a black pen, go over the outlines and then draw 'tangles' you like inside those empty sections. • You may leave your piece in that striking black and white graphic or add color.

COLOR YOUR DESIGN - The example in blue was done using transparent Setacolor textile paints; the yellow/orange one was done using color pencils. To make the color pencils permanent, brush on a layer of textile medium. For all methods, heat set the color using a hot dry iron. Use parchment paper or a Teflon sheet to protect both your work and iron.

QUILT THE POSTCARD - Place the fabric with your drawing face up on top of the stabilizer. Baste the outer edge just to hold it in place while you quilt the piece. Free Motion quilt close to the outlines to make the image really pop. Use your favorite stitch or some of the tangles with your thread work. • Trim the quilted piece to 4" x 6".

ADD A POSTCARD BACKING - I use cardstock for the backs of my postcards. It is easy to write on and can be put through the printer. You may also use fabric for the back. Whichever you choose, be sure to write the word "Postcard" on the back. Cut 4" x 6" pieces for backing. Layer your quilted front and chosen backing together. Using fusible web, fuse the layers together with a dry iron. To finish, ZigZag stitch all around the cut edge.

Mandala Graffiti Quilt

by Jill Buckley

I wanted to create an original design that at first glance appeared to be an abstract design but was interesting enough to compel the viewer to take a closer look. It is hand drawn 'tangles'. I used an ultra-fine tip black Sharpie permanent marker and painted the whole cloth using Setacolor transparent paint.

The design is made up almost entirely of Graffiti lettering and is divided into 12 sections - pie slices - with every other section a mirror image. It reads from the center out and asks the question 'Is it Art or Vandalism?', complete with curly Q question marks.

Jill Buckley

"Being self taught and having no art background or official training means that I do not know what the 'rules' are and I prefer it that way. I work without boundaries or restrictions."

Jill's energetic pieces are "mostly intuitive and derived from simply wanting to know 'What if'..." Jill enjoys exploring endless possibilities. "Having spent many years working in the garment industry, I now find myself truly enjoying the beauty of textiles as art." Explore more of Jill's award winning textile creations by visiting her blog: www.thequiltrat.blogspot.com.

SIZE: 42" x 42"

MATERIALS

Off white cotton fabric - you will be drawing and painting on the fabric
Pebeo Setacolor transparent fabric paint, *Sharpie* ultra-fine black permanent marker
Backing, batting & binding, Sewing machine, needle, thread

Tips for Success:

Pre-wash fabric and stabilize the back with freezer paper. • Experiment with different paints and inks on a scrap before and during the process to avoid making errors on the actual quilt top. • When drawing on fabric, take your time. • Setacolor transparent textile paint allows your pen work to show through. Thinning the paints may cause the color to bleed. • If you use colored pencils, brush a textile medium over the top of the pencil work when you have finished to help "set" the color so that your piece will be washable. • Heat set the finished piece. • Small, tight quilting stitches around and close to the pen work make the lettering stand out. Choose stitch designs that complement the tangles.

Zentangle Crazy Quilt

by Gail Ellspermann

This project is a fun portable one because you can carry a few scraps of fabric and tangle when you have a few minutes during the day. After you have a small collection, join them together to make a colorful quilt that is perfect for a wall decoration or under a vase of flowers.

Give your Zentangle project extra zing by choosing bright colors, but stay away from prints and mottled fabrics - they interfere with your drawn designs.

See basic instructions for drawing 'tangles' on pages 22 - 27.

SIZE: 11" x 13"

MATERIALS

Solid cotton scraps
    (green, yellow, turquoise, lavender)
Bic Mark-It fine point black permanent marker
Black $\frac{1}{4}$" twill tape
Black bias tape for binding
MistyFuse fusible web
Freezer paper as stabilizer
Pressing sheet
Batting, backing & binding
Sewing machine, needle, Black thread

INSTRUCTIONS:

Stabilize fabric by ironing it to the shiny side of freezer paper.
Draw 'tangles' on the fabric using the black marker.
Peel away freezer paper after all drawing is complete.
Place backing fabric wrong side up on an ironing board.
Place quilt batting on backing fabric and add a layer of MistyFuse.
Cut fabric into random geometric shapes.
Arrange on top of MistyFuse, slightly overlapping the edges.
Place a pressing sheet on top. Iron the quilt sandwich to fuse the
    fabric layers together.
Baste the layers together.
Sew Black twill tape to cover overlapped fabric edges. Press.
Square up edges and bind the quilt.

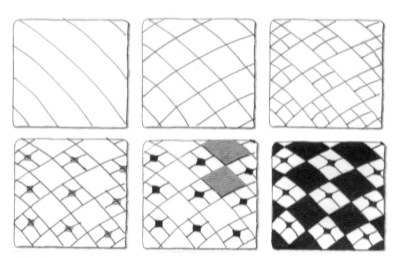

Tartan

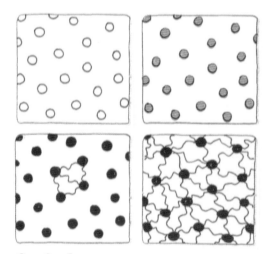

Squiggly

Scan-tastic Quilt with Transfer

by Gail Ellspermann

The magic of technology allows you to transfer your paper Zentangle drawings onto fabric so you can use them to make delicious quilts. You can resize your drawings, combine them with photographs, add text and zoom in on favorite sections of your original.

See basic instructions for drawing 'tangles' on pages 22 - 27.

SIZE: 10" x 20"

MATERIALS
Zentangle drawings on paper
Computer, scanner & printer,
Jacquard Ink Jet Printing Fabric Sheets
Black ½" wide twill tape
Cotton fabric (black and a dark color)
MistyFuse fusible web
Batting, backing & binding
Sewing machine, needle, thread

INSTRUCTIONS:
Place your Zentangle drawing on a computer scanner.
Scan and print the image onto *Jacquard* Ink Jet Printing Fabric.
Quilt Top:
   Place a 3" x 15" dark color center panel right side up on a table.
   Cut Zentangle fabric sheet into rectangles: three 3" x 3", two 1¾" x 3".
   Cut *MistyFuse* rectangles in corresponding sizes.
   Place *MistyFuse* on the center panel, then your Zentangle fabric on top.
   Leave ¼" between the Zentangle pieces.
   Cover with a pressing sheet and use an iron to fuse.
   Cut 3" wide quilt border strips from black fabric
   Stitch strips to the edges of the center panel.
Place backing fabric wrong side up, batting and the top on a table.
Cut 4 strips of twill tape. Position strips around the center panel. Stitch
   through all layers along both edges of the tape.
Free motion quilt meandering lines on the border sections.
Square up the edges and bind the quilt.

Back and Forth

Munchin*   *original Zentangle design

Tangled Postcard and Daisy

by Gail Ellspermann

Transfer Artist Paper is a wonderful product that allows you to draw or print directly and then transfer the image to a number of things, including fabric.

One of the benefits is that you can draw without concern for the inks bleeding in the fabric and leaving fuzzy lines. TAP transfer drawings transfer cleanly allowing for more detailed drawing.

See basic instructions for drawing 'tangles' on pages 22 - 27.

Daisy Mini Quilt

SIZE: $5\frac{1}{2}$" x 8"

MATERIALS
White cotton fabric, batting & backing
Bic Mark-It black permanent marker
Copic colored permanent markers
Lesley Riley fabric•ologie TAP (Transfer Artist Paper)
Assorted sequins & beads
Sewing machine, needle, thread

INSTRUCTIONS:
Using markers, draw an image on Transfer Artist Paper.
Place TAP drawing face down on cotton fabric and follow the
  manufacturer's instructions to transfer the image.
Place backing fabric wrong side up on a table.
Layer batting and the top layer (with your transferred image).
Quilt through all layers, following the lines of the drawing.
Square up the piece to $5\frac{1}{2}$" x 8".
Straight stitch around the piece a scant $\frac{1}{4}$" from the edge.
Zigzag stitch around the edges for added detail.
Embellish with sequins and beads.

Wear this cheerful pin to show your love of Zentangle. This colorful flower brooch is both easy to make and fun to wear as an embellishment.

Flower Pin

SIZE: $4\frac{1}{2}$" diameter

MATERIALS
White cotton fabric (10" square and a scrap)
Bic Mark-It black permanent marker
Copic colored permanent markers
Scrap of cotton batting
Lightweight cardboard, Pin back
Sewing machine, needle, thread

INSTRUCTIONS:
Draw a 2" circle on fabric.
Draw 'tangles' in the circle with markers.
Cut out circle and sew a long Running stitch along the edge.
Cut a $1\frac{1}{2}$" circle from cardboard and cover with a 2" circle of
  batting. Place fabric over batting and pull threads from the
  ends of the Running stitch gently to gather fabric. Tie a knot.
Layer two squares of fabric together, with wrong sides together.
Stitch the edges of the petal shapes together through both layers.
Draw 'tangles' onto the petals.
Cut petals out leaving $\frac{1}{8}$" of raw edge outside of stitching.
Gather the base of petals and stitch around the flower center.
Sew a pin on the back.

By scanning your Zentangle drawings and printing them on fabric you can make multiple postcards to share or swap with friends. It's a great way to expand your collection of Zentangle drawings.

Four coloring methods provide options for achieving different looks using the same "tangle".

The small format makes postcards quick and easy to complete and provides a good base for experimenting with combining techniques.

Have fun!

Gail

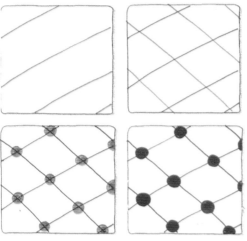

Joints

Postcards with Color

by Gail Ellspermann

I love to draw 'tangles' so I usually just sit down and fill an entire page with images.

To make postcards or Artist Trading Cards (ATCs), simply draw boxes in the size you need then fill the spaces with designs.

Zentangle is both fun and relaxing.

INSTRUCTIONS:
Scan, enlarge & print your Zentangle drawing onto a
    Jacquard Ink Jet Printing Fabric sheet.
Color the printed Zentangle fabric using one of four methods:

Method 1:
    Mix 1 part *Liquitex* Textile Medium with 3 parts of
        Liquitex acrylic paint.
    Use a small paintbrush to apply color to your printed
        Zentangle fabric. Let dry. Peel off backing paper.

Method 2:
    Pour a small amount of three colors of *Lumiere*
        paint onto a paper plate.
    Add a few drops of water to thin the paint.
    Use a foam brush to apply thinned paint to your printed
        Zentangle fabric. Let dry. Peel off backing paper.

Method 3:
    Use a pointed applicator to apply *Tsukineko* All
        Purpose Inks to printed Zentangle fabric.
    Remember that a tiny amount of color goes a long way
        with these inks. Let dry. Peel off backing paper.

Method 4:
    This method gives the finest details.
    Use fine point Bic Mark-It pens to color your printed
        Zentangle fabric. Let dry. Peel off backing paper.

Assembly:
    Cut backing fabric, Timtex and printed Zentangle
        fabric to measure 5" x 7".
    Place backing fabric wrong side up on a table and
        add Timtex stabilizer and Zentangle fabric.
    Stitch through all layers by following the lines of the
        Zentangle design or by free-motion stitching.
    Trim postcard to $4\frac{1}{4}$" x $6\frac{1}{2}$".
    Satin stitch the edges to finish, going around 2-3 times
        for a thicker finished edge.

SIZE: $4\frac{1}{4}$" x $6\frac{1}{2}$"
MATERIALS
Jacquard Ink Jet Printing Fabric Sheets
Zentangle drawings
Bic Mark-It permanent markers
Computer, scanner and printer
5" x 7" cotton fabric for backing
5" x 7" *Timtex* heavy weight interfacing
MistyFuse fusible web
Sewing machine, needle, thread

OPTIONAL COLORING SUPPLIES:
Liquitex Acrylic Paint & *Liquitex* Textile Medium
Jacquard Lumiere paint
Tsukineko All Purpose Ink & applicator
Small paintbrush, Foam paintbrush, Paper plate

Traditional Zentangle for DRAWING...

A very simple ritual is part of every traditional Zentangle.

1. Make a dot in each corner of your paper or piece of fabric with a pencil. Connect the dots to form a border .
2. Lightly draw guideline "strings" with the pencil. The shape can be a zigzag, swirl, X, circle or just about anything that divides the area into sections. It represents the "golden thread" that connects all the patterns and events that run through life. The strings will not be erased but will disappear.
3. Use a black pen to draw Tangles into each section formed by the "string".
4. Rotate the paper or fabric piece as you fill each section with a pattern.

1. Use a pencil to make a dot in each corner.

2. Connect the dots with the pencil.

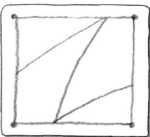

3. Draw a "string" with the pencil as a guideline.
  Try a Z zigzag, a loop, an 'X', or a swirl.

4. Switch to a black pen and draw a tangle pattern in each section formed by the "string". When you cross a line, change the pattern. It is OK to leave some sections blank.

Crescent Moon* *original Zentangle design - Variation
1. Draw curved humps along the inside edges of a section.
2. Draw a curved line on each hump to create arches or moon shapes.
3. Color each moon with black.
4. Draw a continuous curved line inside.
5. Draw additional curved lines to fill the section.

Printemps* *original Zentangle design - Variation
1. Draw a small spiral, sort of like a cinnamon bun or jelly roll. Start with a small "C" shape, then spiral around it and close the end.
2. Make more spirals to fill the section.
3. Add small circles to fill spaces.
4. Color the background with black.

Each Tangle is a unique artistic design and there are hundreds of variations. Start with basic patterns, then create your own.

With Zentangle, no eraser is needed. Just as in life, we cannot erase events and mistakes. Instead, we must build upon them and make improvements from any event.

Life is a building process. All events and experiences are incorporated into our learning process and into our life patterns.

Hollibaugh*
*original Zentangle design - Variation
1. Draw two parallel lines across a section.
2. Rotate the tile then draw another pair of lines letting the shape appear to go "under" the first one.
3. Rotate the tile again and draw another pair of lines that goes behind. Rotate and repeat until the section is filled.
4. Color the background with black if desired.

Static*
*original Zentangle design - Variation
1. Draw a zigzag line from one corner to another.
2. Draw a second zigzag line (Lightening Bolt) parallel to the first one (let the lines join at the ends).
3. Color the zigzag shape with black.
4. Draw on the right side of the black bolt to add an echoing line (don't let the lines join at the ends). Draw additional zigzag lines to fill the section.
5. Turn the tile and draw on the other side of the black bolt to fill the section.
Tip: If you are left-handed, draw on the left side.

Optional... Shading Your Zentangle

Shading adds a touch of dimension.
1. Use the side of a pencil to gently color areas and details with gray.
Suggestions of where to add shading...
• In the center of the Crescent Moon section.
• On one side of each Spiral.
• On the right and left of the first set of parallel lines.
• On the lower zag of each parallel zigzag line.
• Along the edge of some sections to add depth to the
• Along the right edge and the bottom of your finished shape.
• Make shading about $1/8$" wide to "raise" sections off the page.
Note: Use shading sparingly.

Use a pencil to add shading and use a 'paper stump' to rub the pencil areas to smudge, soften and blend the gray shadows.

Traditional Zentangle for DRAWING...

When quilters and stitchers first began to ask me about Zentangle for fabrics, I enthusiastically replied, "What a great idea! Why didn't I think of that?" Originally Zentangle was drawn on paper tiles in black and white. The 'tangles' resemble quilting patterns so many quilters used my books as inspiration for new and exciting fills and backgrounds to finish small decorative quilts.

Fabric artists envisioned small 'tangles' as embellishment to be drawn on fabric with permanent ink. Still others wanted to add color.

Those who love to piece quilts were inspired by the elegant look of black and white. Excitement grew as they added black and white prints to their stash of quilt fabrics, and began to piece them together.

Embroiders wanted to try 'tangles' as accents for designs... sort of like 'Blackwork' but embroidered on fabric rather than counted on woven linen or aida cloth.

To learn even more, I suggest that you purchase a kit or find a class from a CZT (zentangle.com) or add more books to your collection (d-originals.com).

As friends showed me what they were doing, I knew pieces inspired by Zentangle could be an important innovation for fabric artists. Use the basic 'tangles' as inspiration to create your own vision of Zentangle on fabric.

Suzanne

Web

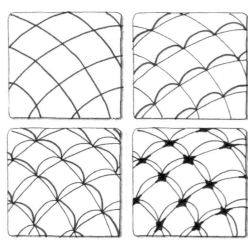

Chillon*

*original Zentangle design

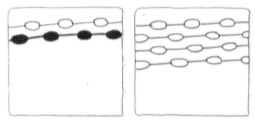

Hotdogs

Flukes*   *original Zentangle design

Cadent*   *original Zentangle design - Variation

Jelly Roll

Swirls

Squiggles 2

Twist & Twirl

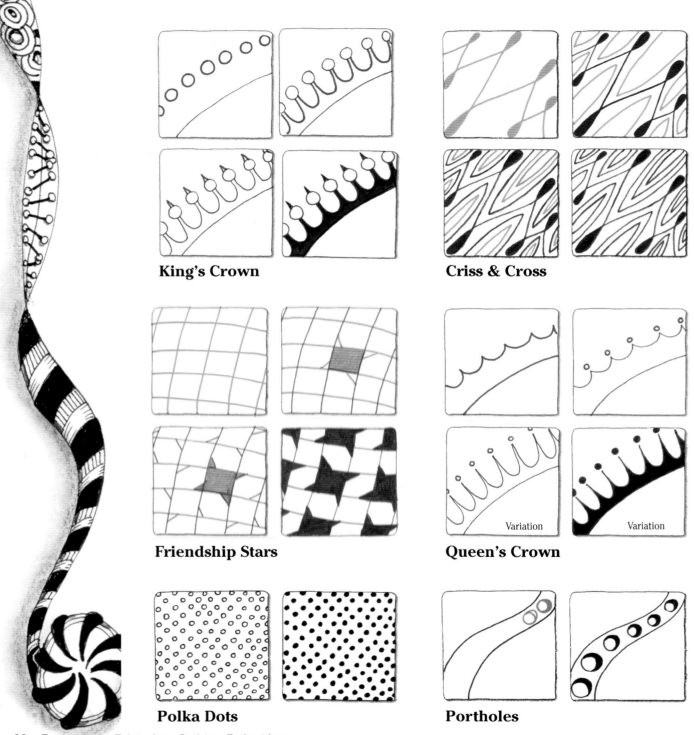

King's Crown

Criss & Cross

Friendship Stars

Queen's Crown

Variation   Variation

Polka Dots

Portholes

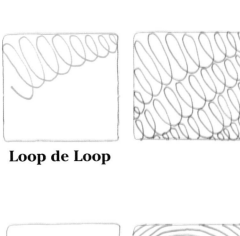

Loop de Loop

Cog Wheel*

*original Zentangle design - Variation

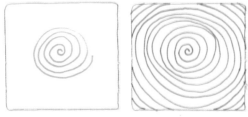

Linked

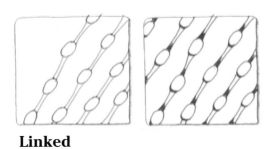

Tiny Pearls

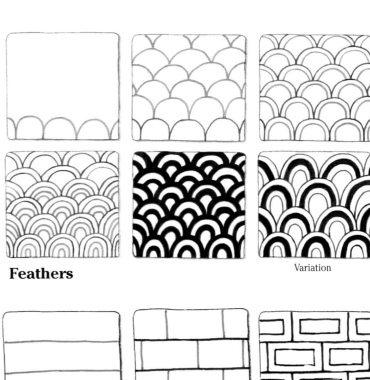

Feathers

Variation

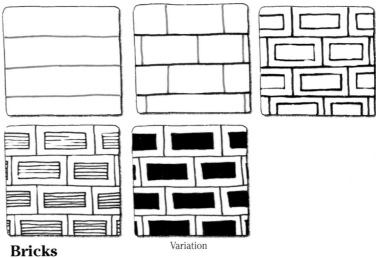

Bricks

Variation

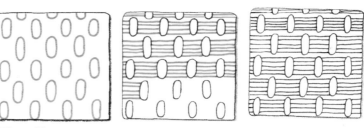

Bundles

Beaded Slipper
by Lauren Horowitz

Hobbit House
by Sherry Pryor

Friendship Blocks

by MaryAnn Scheblein-Dawson, CZT

I was contacted by the Signature Art Quilters, a quilting group from Long Island, NY., inviting me to present a Zentangle lesson at their monthly meeting. Having been a fiber artist long ago, I was intrigued by the possibilities of merging the two art forms.

When I arrived, I was introduced to a group of warm, sharing and creative individuals As you can imagine, their 'show and tell' segment was very inspiring.

During the class, all nine women became so excited about the possibilities that the air was thick with creative energy. After my presentation, these amazing quilters sat together and planned out a Zentangle inspired project. Ten inch squares would be 'tangled'. At one corner, the design must come all the way to the edge. This would allow the patterns to flow from one square to the next when sewn together.

It was an honor to be selected to share my passion for Zentangle and I am proud to present four blocks from their project.

MaryAnn

Sew Zen

by Helene Kusnitz

Zen Stitches

by Mimi Wohlberg

SIZE: 10" x 10"
MATERIALS
Muslin white cotton fabric
Sakura Micron 01 black marker
Batting & backing
Binding if desired
Black thread
Sewing machine, needles
Optional: Embroidery floss, Beads

Quilting, Coloring and Beading (see pages 38 - 39)

INSTRUCTIONS:

Beginning at one corner, use a pencil to lightly draw the 'string' that
separates your block into sections.

Using a black Micron marker, fill in each section with a different 'tangle'.

Layer the backing, batting, and the top.

Quilt on the lines you drew with the marker and add stitching as desired to create
a design that is inspired by Zentangle. TIP: You can either free-motion the
quilting or you can simply hand-guide your machine to stitch the lines.

Embellish with additional embroidery stitches and beads if desired.

FINISHING A QUILT:

Assemble several blocks with black sashing strips between the blocks.

Add a backing and another layer of batting. Bind around the edges.

MaryAnn Scheblein-Dawson

MaryAnn Scheblein-Dawson has a Bachelor of Science Degree in Textile Technology. She has her own business, Paperplay Origami and is an Origami specialist. MaryAnn teaches workshops nationally and internationally. A Certified Zentangle Teacher (CZT), she has added Zentangle to the programs she offers to libraries, schools, museums and craft stores. She also offers in-home lessons. Some of her Zentangle work may be seen in the book "Totally Tangled" by Sandy Steen Bartholomew. View more of MaryAnn's work at www.paperplay-origami.com.

Wandering Tangles

by Sue Needle

"The key to successful free-motion is to relax. Put some music on and don't think! There are no quilt police! Go with the flow - experience the Zen. Just get in the zone and relax!

If you have trouble getting started, do some lines. Once you get comfortable, allow your fabric to move into curves and swirly things. When moving from one area to another, try to vary the density - that's the space between the stitch lines; doing so will give your piece interest."

See basic instructions for free-motion 'tangles' on pages 38 - 39.

SIZE: 12½" x 12½"

MATERIALS
Cotton batik fabric
   (sky blue, light turquoise)
Chalk pencil
Batting, backing & binding
Sewing machine, needle, black thread

INSTRUCTIONS:
Cut the top, batting and backing 13" x 13".
Layer the backing, batting, and top.
Use a chalk pencil to draw the 'string' that divides the piece into sections.
Drop the feed dogs and free-motion quilt 'tangles' in each section.
Cut 2½" border strips and sew to the sides, top and bottom of the piece.
Sew binding to the quilt.

Fireworks   Sunrise

Variations of the same basic stitch

Sue Needle

Sue has been a professional long-arm machine quilter since 1999. She loves the freedom and creativity that quilting offers.

Sue enjoys developing innovative quilting motifs and strives to think outside of the box. Her love of quilting stitches drew her to Zentangle as inspiration for innovative free-motion stitches.

You can see more of Sue's work at www.needlesquilting.com.

Back of the Blue quilt

entangle for Fabric Arts, Quilting, Embroidery

Zentastic Small Quilt

by Sue Needle

To prepare your fabric for free-motion, it is best to pin the layers together around the outside so you won't have to sew around the pins. You can also try a basting spray such as Sulky KK 2000 or a fusible batting. Hobbs has a fusible batting that works well.

It's best to start sewing in the middle and work your way out. This allows you to smooth out any bumps as you go.

See basic instructions for free-motion 'tangles' on pages 38- 39.

SIZE: 18" x 18"
MATERIALS
Black cotton fabric
Chalk pencil
Batting, backing & binding
White thread for quilting
Sewing machine, needle, white thread

INSTRUCTIONS:
Cut the top, batting and backing 24" x 24".
Layer backing, batting, and top.
Use a chalk pencil to draw the string that divides the piece into sections.
Drop the feed dogs and free-motion quilt 'tangles' in each section.
Cut 2½" border strips and sew to the sides, top and bottom of the piece.
Sew binding to the quilt.

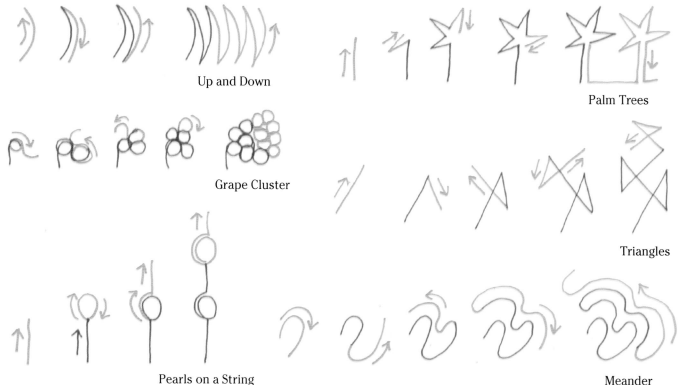

Up and Down

Palm Trees

Grape Cluster

Triangles

Pearls on a String

Meander

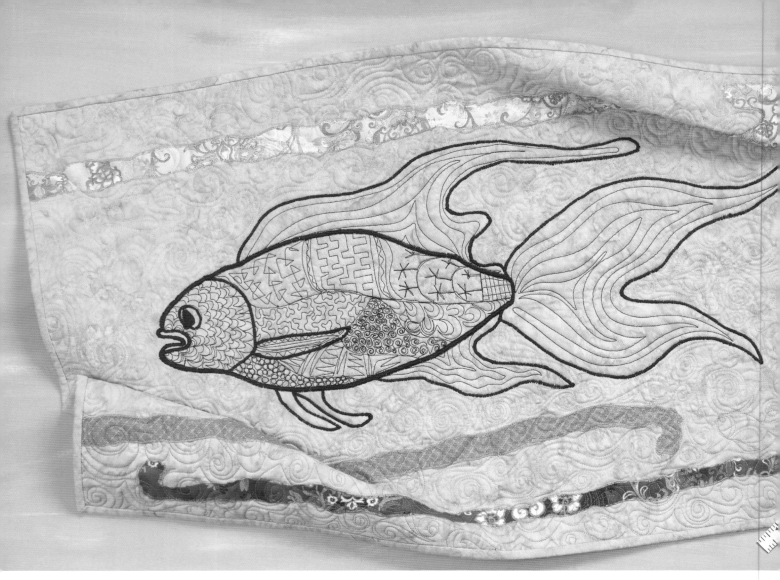

Suzanne McNeill

Suzanne is known as "the Trendsetter" of the craft industry. Dedicated to hands-on creativity, she constantly tests, experiments and invents something new and fun.

She is an artist, designer, columnist, TV personality, publisher, art instructor, author and lover of everything hands-on. Suzanne is the woman behind Design Originals, a publishing company dedicated to all things fun and creative. Visit www.d-originals for a listing of her other books.

To see delightful books, events and a 'Tangle of the Week' visit Suzanne at blog.suzannemcneill.com.

quilted by Sue Needle

The Zen of Fishing

by Suzanne McNeill, CZT

Here's a good example of varying stitch density. There is a lot of space between the stitch lines in the tail, while the eye and fin areas are tightly stitched for effect. To make the design have more punch, I stitched a dark satin stitch outline around the entire fish and fins.

See instructions for 'tangles' on pages 38 - 39.

SIZE: 20½" x 32½"

MATERIALS
Cotton batik fabric (green, blue), Scraps of Blue print fabric
Chalk pencil
Batting, backing & binding
Sewing machine, needle, black thread, green thread

INSTRUCTIONS:
Cut the batting, backing and top, each 21" x 33".
On the green side: Use a chalk pencil to draw a fish and the 'string' that divides the fish
    into sections.
Cut three ½" wide wavy pieces of blue print. Satin stitch above and below the fish as desired.
Layer backing, batting, and top. Baste the layers together.
Satin stitch around the fish, fins and tail with black to make a border.
Drop the feed dogs and free-motion quilt 'tangles' in each section of the fish with
    black thread.
Free-motion quilt the background around the fish with green swirls.
Sew binding to the quilt.

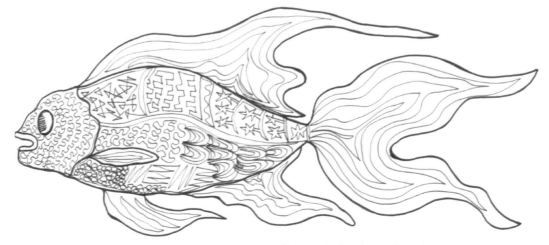

Pat Ferguson lives in the "Quiet Corner" of Connecticut but her quilting studio is anything but quiet. Zentangle and "Zen Quilting" classes are all the rage!

Like Zentangle, "Zen Quilting" takes little time with a minimal amount of materials. Pat challenges her students to create one new piece per week, while journaling their progress. Doing so helps them to watch their progress in both machine quilting and Zentangle design.

SIZE: 7" x 7" (size of design)
MATERIALS
Muslin white cotton fabric, 11" x 11"
Black thread
Batting & backing, 11" x 11"
Black double fold binding
Sewing machine, needles
Optional: Sakura Micron 01 black marker to fill spaces

"Zen Quilting" Blocks
by Patricia Ferguson, CZT

In April 2010, one of my quilting students told me about Zentangle. That very day I spent six hours on the www.zentangle.com website and was completely transformed. I was already familiar with the Sakura Micron fine pigment pens used in Zentangle because I had them amongst my quilting supplies for making labels for the back of my quilts.

With Zentangle, I could now create fantastic little works of art and these drawings opened up a whole new world for me with my machine quilting techniques.

INSTRUCTIONS:

Zentangle patterns fill odd shaped spaces with beautiful designs, much like machine quilting fills odd shaped spaces with beautiful background stitching.

So off I went, searching for Zentangle designs that I could convert and adapt to continuous line quilting. I now have many more unique background fillers that take me far and beyond traditional stippling designs.

This exciting new art form lead to me become a CZT (Certified Zentangle Teacher) and then to combine those skills with quilting to create "Zen Quilting" classes for my students. Although I am a longarm quilter, I still need to stay connected to my domestic machine for teaching purposes. Creating these tiny machine quilted masterpieces, keeps my skills sharpened and enables me to remain one with my machine."

Each design is 7" square or twice the size of a standard 3½" Zentangle paper tile. True to Zentangle form, the quilted pieces can be viewed with any side up or down.

CORNERS FOR FLEXIBLE HANGING:

I devised a flexible way to hang and rotate each piece. To accomplish this, I cut four 4" fabric squares. I folded each square on the diagonal, positioned one in each corner then added traditional double fold binding around the piece. These little "pockets" allow me to insert a flat dowel (with a bulldog hanger attached) into any two corners.

Patricia Ferguson

Pat has been teaching and machine quilting on a domestic machine since 1985 and longarm quilting since 2004. Her award winning quilts have been featured in various publications. She is a proud member of Studio Art Quilt Associates (saqa.org), Artists Open Studios of Northeast Connecticut (aosct.org), and three quilt guilds. She is also a member of International Machine Quilters Association (IMQA) and contributing writer for their "On Track" quarterly publication.

Pat's "Zen Dahlia" quilt won a Purple Ribbon and Viewer's Choice Award at the 2010 NBQA quilt show.

Visit www.patfergusonquilts.com to find out more about Pat's quilts, trunk shows, classes, and online store. You can contact her at pat@patfergusonquilts.com.

DRAWING and QUILTING

One method of Zentangle on fabric is to combine drawing with stitching. Most of the sample blocks on pages 28 - 29 use this combo technique.

Using a regular sewing machine, you can either free-motion the quilting or you can simply topstich the lines with a regular sewing machine. Embellish your block with additional stitches and beads if desired.

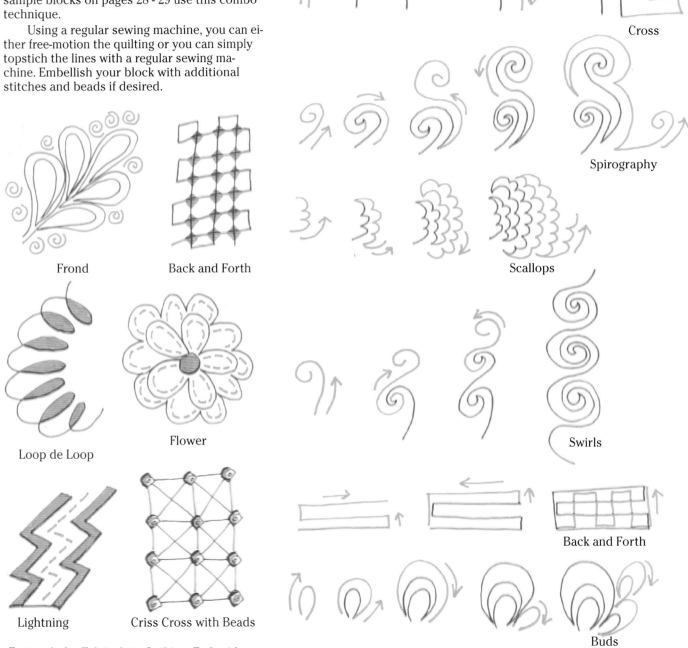

Cross

Frond

Back and Forth

Spirography

Loop de Loop

Flower

Scallops

Lightning

Criss Cross with Beads

Swirls

Back and Forth

Buds

FREE-MOTION STITCHES

Drop the feed dogs and free-motion quilt 'tangles' in each section. Connect and create new patterns as you go.

Growth

Up, Down and Across

Swirly

Leaves

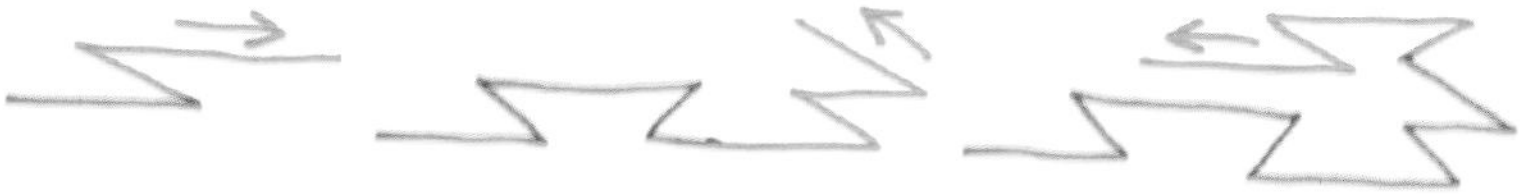

Primitive

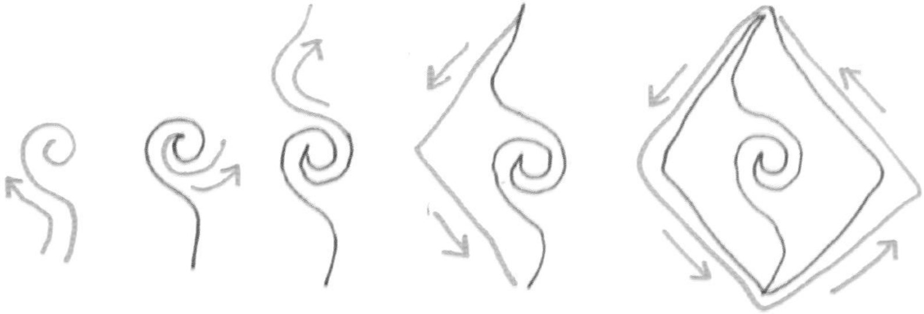

Swirl in a Box

Borders & Fillers

These patterns can be used as borders, or by repeating several rows, they look great as filler. Simpler to make than some swirly designs, they stitch up quickly but look intricate on a quilt.

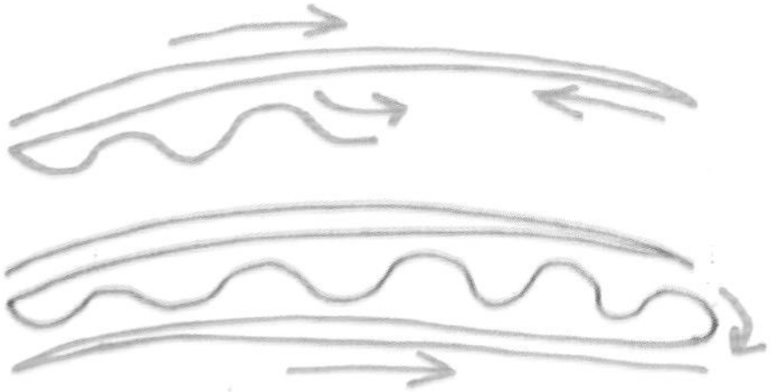

Serpentine

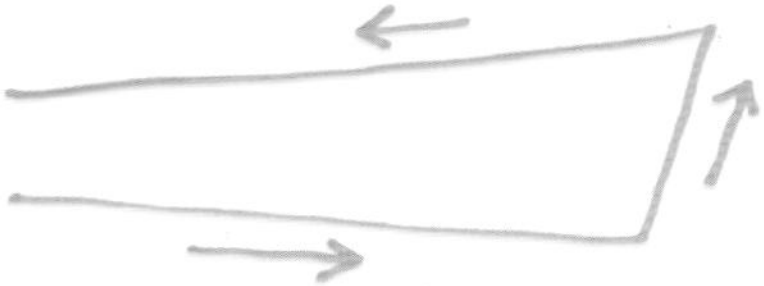

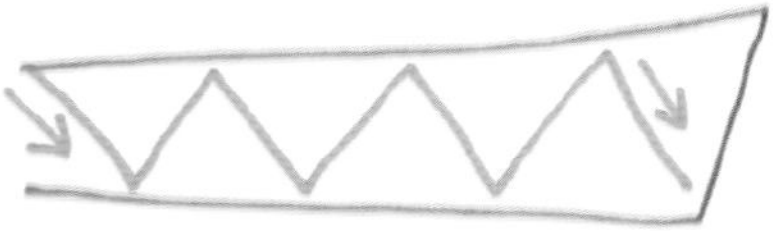

Peaks

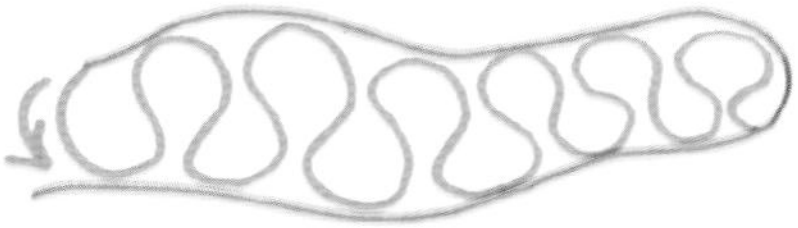

Serpentine 2

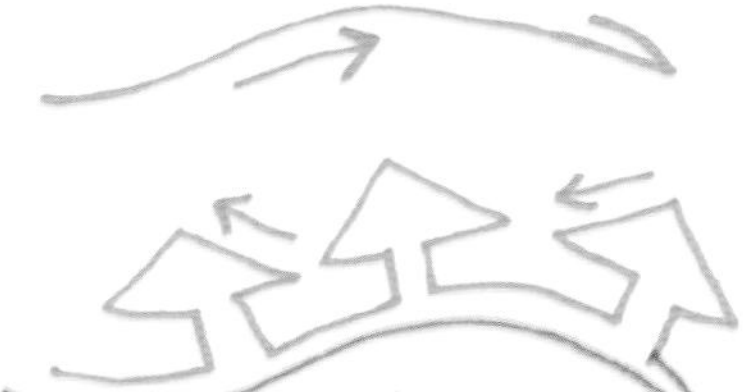

Arrows

Little Blocks

by Vicki Murray, CZT

My goal in doing this project was to show people that you don't have to be a professional quilter or have a fancy embroidery machine to create awesome pieces.
I used a regular sewing machine, a few decorative stitches and sumptuous Sulky threads.
See basic instructions for machine stitched 'tangles' on pages 38 - 39.

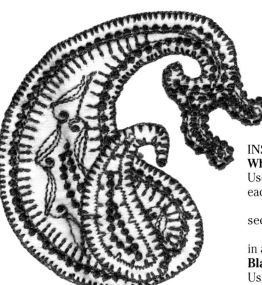

Use decorative machine stitches at random to create a design that is inspired by Zentangle.

SIZE: 24" x 24"

MATERIALS
Solid cotton fabric (black, white)
Wash-away stabilizer • Wash-away blue marker
Sulky 12 weight 100% cotton thread (ivory, black)
Topstitch needle • Bobbin weight thread in the bobbin
Batting, backing and binding • Optional: Black piping
Chalk pencil • Sewing machine, needle

INSTRUCTIONS:
White Squares: Cut 12 squares, 5" x 5". Fuse stabilizer to the back. Use a blue marker to draw a $3\frac{1}{2}$" x $3\frac{1}{2}$" section in the center of each square. Sew decorative machine stitches in 10 of the squares.

Use the blue marker to draw 9 small squares in 2 of the $3\frac{1}{2}$" sections. Stitch a 'Paradox' tangle (page 42) in each section.

Note: In one section, all Paradox' tangles rotate the same way; in another section, adjacent tangles rotate in opposite directions.

Black Center: Cut 1 square 13" x 13". Fuse stabilizer to the back. Using a chalk pencil, draw an 8" pentagon (with 5 sides) in the center. Draw a smaller 4" pentagon in the center.

Starting at a star point, stitch variations of 'Paradox' tangles (page 42) with ivory thread. Note: In the pentagons, adjacent 'Paradox' tangles are stitched in opposite rotations to form 'fans'.

Assembly: Cut all 12 squares (with decorative stitches) to $4\frac{3}{4}$" x $4\frac{3}{4}$".
White Sashing: Cut $1\frac{3}{4}$" x $4\frac{3}{4}$". Fuse stabilizer to the back. Sew decorative machine stitches.
White Borders: Cut $1\frac{3}{4}$" wide by length needed. Fuse stabilizer to the back. Sew decorative machine stitches as desired.
Finishing: Sew the top together using piping (optional) between the white pieces. Layer the top, batting and backing. Quilt the top. Sew binding to the quilt.

Vicki Murray

For over 50 years, Vicki has done it all - quilting, sewing, crochet, knitting, beading... and now Zentangle! "I started tangling a little over a year ago, but before that, I never even doodled. Creating 'tangles' is a whole new experience and I am completely obsessed! I love the challenge of translating tangles onto fabric."

You can see more of Vicki's work at okztfans.wetpaint.com.

MACHINE STITCHES

Think creatively.

Use variations of the zig zag stitch and put together decorative machine stitches to create a design that is inspired by Zentangle.

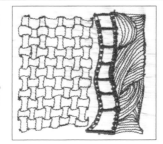
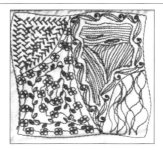
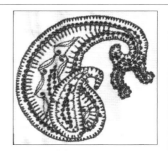

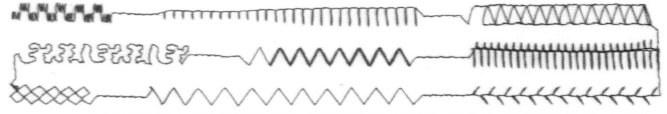

Hand Guided MACHINE STITCHES

Be imaginative.

Use a Straight stitch to sew and hand-guide your layered fabric piece to create quilted 'tangles'.

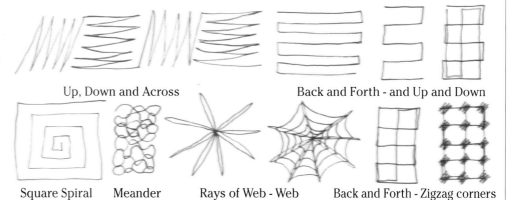

Up, Down and Across   Back and Forth - and Up and Down

Square Spiral   Meander   Rays of Web - Web   Back and Forth - Zigzag corners

Rick's 'Paradox'

*original Zentangle design - Variation

Note: The 3½" section uses 9 squares of 'Paradox'.

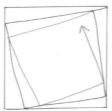

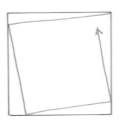

A single square of 'Paradox'.

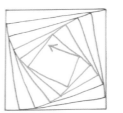
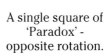

A single square of 'Paradox' - opposite rotation.

Handy Tangles Block

by Brenda Zangre

SIZE: 9½" x 9½"

MATERIALS
Cotton white muslin fabric
Fusible lightweight stabilizer
Pencil
Batting & backing
Sewing machine, needle, black thread

INSTRUCTIONS:
Draw hands on muslin.
Fuse stabilizer to the back of the fabric.
Sew on the lines with a Zigzag stitch.
Fill in with 'tangles'.
Layer the top, backing and batting.
Sew around the edge leaving a 6"
    opening for turning.
Turn the piece right side out. Press.
Sew the opening closed.
Quilt over the Zigzag stitch around
    the hands.

Here's a fun idea for a design. Trace around your hand, your child's hand, or an old glove to get a variety of hand sizes. Wouldn't it be fun to record the hands of your whole family or the soccer team? How about your bible class or art club?

Lend a hand and make a quilt for Meals on Wheels or your favorite philanthropic organization to auction at their next charity drive.

Bleach Discharge Quilt

by patsy monk, CZT

Discharge creates a design by removing color from a dark surface. This intriguing bleach process creates a unique result every time.

SIZE: 20" x 20"

MATERIALS
Black cotton fabric
Freezer paper as stabilizer
Soft Scrub® and/or Bleach pen
Batting, backing & binding
Thread (black, white)
Sewing machine, needle

If needed, enlarge your design on a copy machine. Using a light table or window, trace design onto the non-waxy side of freezer paper using a fine Sharpie black permanent marker. • Fuse a piece of freezer paper to the back of your fabric as stabilizer. To secure the freezer paper to fabric, sew around the piece using a basting stitch. • Using a medium stitch length, sew on all the lines with white thread. The stitching lines are guides to applying the bleach.

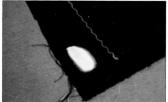

There are 2 ways to bleach: *Soft Scrub* or a Bleach pen. *Soft Scrub* tends to stay put and gives a well defined line. Because the bleach pen contains more liquid, it tends to bleed and spread much faster. To use *Soft Scrub*, pour a small amount into a glass container. If the *Soft Scrub* is not fresh, add a few drops of bleach and stir well. Paint *Soft Scrub* on with a small, inexpensive brush. • Test each method on a scrap of similar fabric to determine which method you prefer and to evaluate the bleed. Not all fabric will discharge nicely. • Using the method you prefer, paint the entire piece. On some areas, you will need to let the bleach dry and come back later to paint more. After painting the entire piece, let it dry. • In each section, paint on your choice of 'tangles' with a bleach pen using a very light touch. When you finish bleaching, leave the stabilizer on the back. (If you retouch an area with more bleach, you will need the paper for support. The paper will dry with the pressing of the fabric.) Hand wash the piece in water, rinsing it thoroughly. Press it dry and examine it. If you are very light in your application of the bleach, you may need to retouch an area with bleach and repeat the wash-press step. Once you are happy with the work, remove all freezer paper and all stitches. Machine wash with water only to be sure you have removed all the bleach. Dry and press. Layer the top, batting and backing. Quilt around the tangle lines. Bind the edges of the quilt.

patsy monk

"Creative energy is healing energy and that's what drives my art", shared patsy.

It is obvious that patsy is an amazing craftsperson. She loves everything handmade and pursues her passions in an energetic and creative manner. She teaches classes and especially loves to incorporate her nursing background into everyday living. "My love for repetitive patterns is reflected in my hobbies. I quilt, knit, weave, create glass beads and tangle. If it moves slowly enough, tangle it! "

You can see more of patsy's work at www.monkink.com.

Crazy Patchwork

by Ellyn Sheidlower

You don't have to worry about raw edges with this crazy patch because they are hidden beneath the bias tape and the border strips.

SIZE: 11" x 11"
MATERIALS
White cotton fabric
8 assorted black and white
    cotton prints
Freezer paper
Fusible web
Batting, backing & binding
Sewing machine, needle, thread

INSTRUCTIONS:
Cut squares for the top, batting and backing. Cut each to 12" x 12".
Cut freezer paper to 12" x 12". On the non-waxy side, draw the 'strings' that divide the square into sections to be pieced.

FABRIC PATCHES:
Decide which fabric will be used in each area, label the areas on the freezer paper with a black pen. Cut out the freezer paper sections to use as templates.
Apply fusible web to the back of each fabric. Cut out the shapes using the freezer paper templates.
Position the shapes on the top and fuse in place.

BIAS TAPE:
Choose 3 different prints and make 16" of bias tape from each one.
Make your own bias tape by folding a square of fabric on the diagonal and cutting (I used ½" wide strips) parallel to the diagonal line. Making your own bias allows you to choose the width.
Fold each side inward to make a folded edge on each side. Press the strip centering the raw edges. Lay the bias tape between the patches with the raw side down. Cover both raw edges with bias tape.
Hand stitch or topstich in place.

FINISHING:
Cut a 1" white border and sew to the sides, top and bottom of the square. Press.
Layer the top, backing and batting.
Square up the piece to 12" x 12".
Sew around the edge leaving a 6" opening for turning.
Turn the piece right side out. Press. Sew the opening closed.
Quilt as desired.

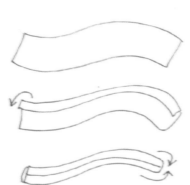

Make your own decorative
bias tape from strips of fabric.

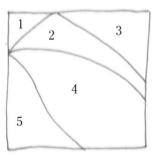

Draw divisions on
smooth freezer paper.

Position shapes, fuse in
place.

Cover edges wih bias
tape, stitch in place.

Add a 1" border on each
side of the square.

Crazy Patch Block

by Jennifer Lokey

Use your embroidery skills to sew thread designs that look just like the tangles you draw with a pen! Zentangle enthusiasts, quilters and hand-sewers will appreciate the relaxing calm that descends when you sew these simple shapes. French knots fill spaces just like dots, but they have an extra dimension. Experiment with Running stitches and Stem stitches for a beautiful result.

SIZE: 16" x 16"
MATERIALS
Cotton fabric (solid black, solid white,
    black-white prints)
Black bias tape
Freezer paper as a template
Water soluble blue pen
Embroidery floss (black, white)
Fusible web
Batting, backing & binding
Sewing machine, needle, black thread

INSTRUCTIONS:
Cut freezer paper to 16" x 16".
On the non-waxy side, draw the 'strings' that divide the square into sections.
Decide which fabric to use in each area, label the areas on freezer paper.
Cut out the areas and use as templates for cutting your fabrics.
Apply fusible web to the back of solid and print fabric scraps. Cut out
    the shapes using the freezer paper templates.
Cut the top, batting and backing to 16" x 16".
Position the shapes in the center of the top and fuse in place.
Cover the edges with black bias tape.
Lightly mark the stitch lines as desired with a water soluble blue pen.
Embroider with black floss on white spaces and white floss on black spaces.
Layer backing, batting, and top. Baste the layers together.
Quilt on the bias tape.
Square up the piece to 16" x 16". Sew binding to the edges of quilt.

Jennifer Lokey

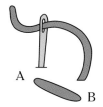

"I have been designing quilts and patterns for 25 years. I have been drawing and doodling for most of my life. Recently I discovered that my meandering line drawings could be more professional and have a name – "Zentangle". Combining my passions has allowed me to experience a new dimension of 'What If'."

Jennifer loves sharing her discoveries and spreading the joy of quilting with others. One of her passions is combining multiple techniques. This lovely piece involves piecing with printed fabrics. Then Jennifer added large embroidery stitches in areas of the quilt to add fabulous texture and depth.

Stem Stitch
Work from left to right to make regular, slanting stitches along the stitch line. Bring the needle up above the center of the last stitch. Also called 'Outline' stitch.

Straight Stitch
Come up at A and go down at B to form a simple flat stitch. Use this stitch for hair for animals and for simple petals on small flowers.

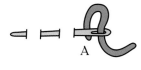

Running Stitch
Come up at A. Weave needle through the fabric, making short, even stitches. Use this stitch to gather fabrics, too.

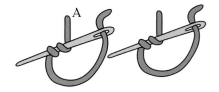

French Knot
Come up at A. Wrap the floss around the needle 2 to 3 times. Insert the needle close to A. Hold the floss and pull the needle through loops gently.

38 Patterns for DRAWING...

Swirly - Whirly
page 5

Frond
page 5

W2*
page 7

Keeko*
page 7

Bubbles
page 9

Cubine*
page 9

Knightsbridge*
page 11

Squiggly
page 15

Tartan
page 15

Back and Forth
page 17

Munchin*
page 18

Joints
page 20

Crescent Moon*
page 22

Printemps*
page 22

Hollibaugh*
page 23

Static*
page 23

Web
page 24

Chillon*
page 24

Hotdogs
page 24

Flukes
page 25

Jelly Roll
page 25

Squiggles 2
page 25

Cadent*
page 25

Swirls
page 25

Twist & Twirl
page 25

King's Crown
page 26

Friendship Stars
page 26

Polka Dots
page 26

Criss & Cross
page 26

Queen's Crown
page 26

Portholes
page 26

Loop de Loop
page 27

Cog Wheel*
page 27

Linked
page 27

Tiny Pearls
page 27

Feathers
page 27

Bricks
page 27

Bundles
page 27

Free-Motion Quilting
page 38 - 39

Machine
Stitching
page 42

30 Patterns for FREE-MOTION QUILTING...

Fireworks-Sunrise
page 33

Up and Down
page 35

Grapes
page 35

Pearls on a String
page 35

Palm Trees
page 35

Triangles
page 35

Meander
page 35

Frond
page 38

Back and Forth
page 38

Loop de Loop
page 38

Flower
page 38

Lightning
page 38

Criss Cross with Beads
page 38

Cross
page 38

Spirography
page 38

Scallops
page 38

Swirls
page 38

Back and Forth
page 38

Buds
page 38

Growth
page 39

Up, Down and Across
page 39

Swirly
page 39

Leaves
page 39

Primitive
page 39

Swirl in a Box
page 39

Serpentine
page 39

Peaks
page 39

Serpentine 2
page 39

Arrows
page 39

Bleach
pages 44 - 45

Crazy Patch
pages 46 - 47

Embroidery
pages 48 - 49